BROKEN yet Restored
MY FAITH SET ME FREE

SHARITA WOODWARD

Broken Yet Restored: My Faith Set Me Free!

Copyright 2020 © Sharita Woodward

All rights reserved. No part of this publication may be reproduced, stored in a retrieval system, or transmitted in any form or by any means—for example, electronic, photocopy recording—without the prior written permission of the publisher. The only exception is for brief quotations in printed reviews.

Published by ELOHAI International Publishing & Media
P.O. Box 64402
Virginia Beach, VA 23467
ElohaiPublishing.com

Connect with the author @SharitaWoodward on Instagram.

Scripture quotations are from the ESV® Bible (The Holy Bible, English Standard Version®), copyright ©2001 by Crossway, a publishing ministry of Good News Publishers. Used by permission. All rights reserved.

Scripture quotations from The Authorized (King James) Version. Rights in the Authorized Version in the United Kingdom are vested in the Crown. Reproduced by permission of the Crown's patentee, Cambridge University Press.

ISBN: 978-0-9981249-9-5
Printed in the United States of America

Dedication

I want to first dedicate this book to my granny Pastor and Overseer, Novella Christine McLauchlin! She planted the seed of God in me at a very young age and never stopped watering it. She encouraged me to write my story but didn't make it to see the final version. For you Granny, I promise to carry the torch and spread the word of God, to preach the gospel unapologetically and not be afraid! I love you forever.

I also dedicate this book to God. He stayed by my side and He kept me. Even though I walked through the valley, He was right there. When I fell, He caught me and stood me up. He's in me and for that, I will never fail. Next, I dedicate this book to my father, Thornell Mclauchlin Jr. who taught me the importance of foundation and the definition of real love. I'm forever grateful for him. Lastly, my daughter Davia Morgan, because without you I probably would not have survived. You came and gave me PURPOSE!

Acknowledgements

I would like to thank my family for staying solid and supporting me even when you learned about all this just six months before I released the book. To my mother for being a STRONG, BLACK QUEEN. To my twin, Nita, who stood by my side the entire time. My eldest sister Sherrell for teaching me how to be a woman on a different level. My brothers who protect me and ride for me. I would like to thank the man in my life: thank you for loving me right. Thanks for being patient with me. Thanks for loving my daughter like your own.

    To you all, thanks for helping me experience a life that I wouldn't have believed could be mine if someone would have told me this ten years ago. I LOVE YOU ALL!!!!

Contents

Part 1: In Love

My Pain Stained Me.	9
Chapter 1: Foundation	13
Chapter 2: Spoil me, I Like That...	19
Chapter 3: Abandoned Dreams	23
Chapter 4: I Can't believe He's So Controlling!	29
Chapter 5: Everything has changed!	33
Chapter 6: Be Patient, Pray!	39
Chapter 7: Too Many Battles	43
Chapter 8: No Judgement Zone	47

PART 2: Thoughts on Paper

Chapter 9: Confused… Where is This Going?	55
Chapter 10: Guide Me Until I'm Sure!	57
Chapter 11: There's So Much More Still Worth Fighting For!	61

Chapter 12: Do it with Tears in your Eyes.   65
Do it Afraid!

Chapter 13: God Please Help Me!!!   71

Chapter 14: You Cannot Allow Fear to Setup   73
in Your Mind

Chapter 15: Cycles   77

Chapter 16: Don't look back!   83

Chapter 17: Falling in Love All Over Again   87

Chapter 18: The Altar   89

Chapter 19: Three Years Later,   93
Still Rebuilding... Patience.

Chapter 20: Watch God!   97

Chapter 21: I'll Never Leave You nor Forsake You   105

Part 1:
In Love

My Pain Stained Me

Why am I here yet again?
Tears running down my face.
My heart aching and crying out to God.
I've grown, or so I thought. I just knew I would now be able to see the signs that once blindsided me.
Are there really issues that I've ignored?
Am I exactly where I should be right now?
It has to be, because here I am.
On the floor, in the closet, crying my eyes out.
Praying to God to heal my broken heart.
I hate feeling like this… broken, bruised, battered... *again*.
Could it be that I give too much of me without any deposits made back into me? Now I am emotionally in the negative due to too many withdrawals. Now my heart has insufficient emotional funds.
Either way, I vowed to never be in this place again.
I told myself I would guard my heart above all things and not allow it to feel this type of heartbreak.
Am I not in control of my feelings? How could I be when

BROKEN YET RESTORED

God is in control of it all? I really want to understand this place where I am, so I'm trying hard to understand why I've arrived here and how did I get here in the first place. I guess my head was so far in the clouds I didn't even realize what truly existed here on solid ground.

Is it possible I'm responsible for the pain I feel? Or is it meant to make me stronger? They say once something is broken it mends back together stronger than before. If that's the case, my heart must be made of steel.

My heart is an essential organ so it's detrimental that I value it. It's come down to my heart for his or His! Help me Father. I don't want my heart to become hardened. Teach me how to love, and even more importantly, please show me how to love people the way they should be loved. My heart is genuine and fragile. I don't want to become so guarded that I'll never be able to love again. I just want to be healed so that my pain won't interfere with how I love. Is it really true you can love someone and still hurt them? What kind of love is that? Or is it simply a control mechanism? I love myself. I know my worth. I just don't want to lose the ability to love and trust. Speaking of trust, how do you gain trust for someone you love after betrayal?

Is that even possible?

I know God has a plan for me; I just pray I stay out of God's way and allow His will to be done in my life. Every time I move in my own will, my soul takes an extreme punishment. Allow me to be led by you, God! Purify my heart

and allow my soul to be free. Allow me to trust you Lord because I have to in order to do your will. Allow me to truly forgive. God I'm broken before you, and I thank you in advance for placing grace over my broken heart!
I SURRENDER!

BROKEN YET RESTORED

Chapter 1: *Foundation*

"For the Lord God is a sun and shield; the Lord bestows favor and honor. No good thing does he withhold from those who walk uprightly." - Psalm 84:11

Strong, independent, and fearless. Ready to take on the world. Yes! That is how I would have described myself as I packed up and moved out of my parents' house at the young age of seventeen. I put college on hold to start a future with my new boyfriend Warren Lewis. I just knew this relationship would be perfect. Everyone in my family was against it and no one gave me their blessing, but *hey, what do they know?* I reasoned. This is my life, my journey, and Warren and I are in love.

Prior to dating Warren, I was a salad bar manager at a local grocery store. I didn't have a lot of responsibility per se', however I made my family's responsibilities my own. My focus was on work and helping my mom pay bills, because my father had gotten sick and was not able to work.

BROKEN YET RESTORED

My father *always* held down the household. He *always* worked, and on his days off, he was *always* with us. He took ALL of his six children to our dentist and doctor visits. We visited local parks and playgrounds most Sundays when we were younger, and he took us for late-night rides. We listened to oldies but goodies on Washington DC's 102.3 FM. I remember I couldn't wait to turn thirty so I could get a "Thirty and Over Club Card," which the radio station gave to its listeners for entry into all the hottest events. Now I'm thirty-three and can care less about that club card.

    I gained a strong foundation in family, love, and hard work from my father. My father loved to build things. He built his own race car when he was younger, and I have heard the story sooo many times, because he tells everyone he comes in contact with about his hand-built race car. I always wanted to be with my father when I was younger so I could learn how to build things just like him. Seeing him down messed me up pretty badly. In addition to seeing my mother hustle hard to pay the bills, which was once primarily my pops' responsibility, I had to help my mother hold down our household. She was and still is my Queen. So I worked, hustled, and did what was necessary to help keep our family afloat.

    I met Warren during the late summer when he began calling my house every day. He was the cousin of my twin sister's boyfriend. He had gotten my number from his cousin. Warren didn't have my cell phone number, just the house phone, so he called for at least two weeks before we actually had a real conversation. My mother said he would call and hang up when I wasn't home. I thought that was very rude of him and couldn't wait to actually catch his call so I could tell him that I didn't appreciate his behavior. I didn't know his number, because he always blocked it when he called the house.

One day, I was home and answered Warren's call. I asked him why he had continuously called and hung up on my mother. He gave me some story, and although I still thought his actions were rude, I let it slide. We moved past that and talked for hours. We finally met one Saturday in September. It was a beautiful day. He told me he was on his way and I was so excited that I began walking up the street. When I saw this tan, beat-up van roll down the street, I remember thinking, *I hope this isn't him!* He slowed down, and I kept walking, trying my best to ignore him, because I did not want to be seen in that thing. My face gave me away. He knew I was a twin and stopped that loud van right beside me. I couldn't turn around or ignore him or I'd seem stuck-up, so I reluctantly hopped in. We rode around in his van for hours, smoking, laughing, and getting to know each other.

It's funny because when he called to tell me he was coming near my house, I was actually on the phone talking to my then boyfriend, D. My twin sister hated that relationship because she said we were more like phone buddies if anything. I didn't care about that. D and I knew everything about one another and I felt so good talking to him. Warren, however, had me second guessing that feeling. After hours of riding around and talking, I did something I had never done before. As I was getting out of the van, I said, "Warren, be my boyfriend!"

"Yes."

"Are you serious?"

"Yes," he said.

With that, I kissed him, and I climbed out of the van…

I grew up in Riverdale, Maryland during the eighties. The atmosphere outside of my home consisted of gangs, prostitutes, fights, hood love, recreational centers, ambitious children, and hustlers—and the hustlers are what I remember the most. I was amazed at the amount of money they flashed around as they bragged outside near our home. When I was ten years old, I remember one incident so clearly. One day, when my brother Joe and I walked to the corner store at the front of our neighborhood, the OGs (original gangstas' or older hustlers) of the neighborhood were shooting dice right by the entrance to the complex and next to the store. All of our friends were already at the store. In fact, everyone had money except Joe and I. I asked if anyone could buy me a doughnut stick, and everyone said "no." I became so mad and left the store. On our way back home, I was still upset, but soon my mood changed. Despite the fact that the block was packed when we walked inside the store, on the way home it was empty, like a ghost town. I thought my eyes were playing tricks on me when I saw it. Money EVERYWHERE.

FOUNDATION

Apparently, the police had come and the illegal drug dealers were caught off guard. They ran from the block quickly and left the money right there as the police chased them up the street. I gathered up every dollar they had left behind and went back to the store VERY happy. I bought everything my brother and I wanted. When my friends saw us running back into the store with money, they asked me where I got the money and if I could buy them something too. The tables had turned just that quickly.

My parents wanted better for us so they moved us out of the "hood" and into the suburbs, which was a drastic change for me. My new view now consisted of railroad tracks, horses, and woods… lots of woods. The move messed me up badly, and I was out of my element, or so I thought. I remember feeling like I was suffocating, so eventually, I did what I knew would make me feel back at home. I grabbed some "work" and hit the block. I took over that nice quiet little neighborhood. I had people coming from different areas just to get what I had. I was making money. During this time, I learned a lot and had a lot of experiences with my square roots family. I met people that became family for life.

I had finished high school and received my high school diploma shortly after meeting Warren, so I felt my future was limitless. Warren and I had been together for eight months, and we'd been talking about moving into our own place since practically day one. (This was a red flag I didn't notice.) I was anxious and excited to start my life with him.

BROKEN YET RESTORED

When it came time for me to move, I just thought that all our relationship needed to survive was love, loyalty, and money to pay our bills. This was soooo far from the truth. Since Warren was one of the highest-paid hustlers on the block, he didn't have a care in the world, and as his girl, neither did I. In our new place, our rent would only be $1,000 a month. I knew we'd be fine. Warren and I were in love so deeply, and we couldn't stay away from one another. We would do anything to make our new living arrangement work. What could possibly go wrong? I was determined to be with him. My love and I would live together regardless of whether my family approved.

Chapter 2: *Spoil me, I like that...*

It's important to know the relationship we have with money, before getting into romantic relationships with people.

"If you're cool, then I'm cool, and we're cool." Anthony Hamilton's "Cool" ringtone sang through my cell phone, and I smiled from ear-to-ear knowing who was on the other end. Just hearing Warren's ringtone sent butterflies through my stomach.

"Hey baby," I blushed as I paced my room floor. "Come downstairs; I have something for you." I was so happy. Warren gave me random surprises almost daily. I hung up so fast and dashed for the door.

Financial security was a desire for me. During my childhood, after I turned eight, it was financially rough for my family. I didn't get any Christmas gifts, nor did I enjoy the luxury of back-to-school shopping or birthday gifts. My mom and dad had six kids back-to-back, so our household became tight REAL fast. On holidays and special events, we had to "understand." Understand meant that there wasn't enough money to take care of the household, provide what we needed, and still splurge for holiday presents. Some nights we had to go to bed without food and wait until we got to school to eat breakfast. More times than not, my mother would make us all food. The six of us would eat our meals then eat our mom's food. My mom has always been a selfless, caring, and amazing woman so she would share all of her food with us. We didn't have much money, but our home was filled with love, laughter, discipline, morals, and values. As our family grew larger, we no longer received many gifts, but our household had more than enough love to go around.

When Warren came into my life, he showered me with gifts: including jewelry, clothes, shoes—you name it—he gave it to me. His generosity made me feel "loved." It reminded me of when I was five years old and my parents bought the entire Barbie aisle from the toy store and made the third bedroom in our apartment a life-size Barbie room. My sisters and I had EVERYTHING Barbie. That was an amazing feeling for a five-year-old girl.

"Here you go baby, just because I love you." Warren had given me four pair of shoes, three outfits, and a gold necklace.

"I love you baby," I said as I hugged him tightly.

"I love you, too," he said as he leaned in and gave me

SPOIL ME, I LIKE THAT...

the famous forehead kiss. "Well I have to get going. I have to be somewhere in fifteen minutes. I just wanted to brighten your day and see you smile."

"Now go put on something nice and do something fun. I'll catch up with you later," he said.

Warren came to see me often. Sometimes his visits were quick, and I got used to his routine. He'd call, tell me he was on the way to my job or house, and each time without fail, he had something nice for me. His giving heart and sexy smile won me over. On other occasions, we'd sit in the parking lot of my job or my parents' community and we'd talk for hours.

That day, the smile on my face couldn't have been any wider if someone pulled my face back. I walked back upstairs with big bags and a smile to match. Nobody could tell me anything!

I spent most nights with Warren at the place he shared with my sister's boyfriend. We would have so much fun and he treated me like a queen. He opened doors, brought my favorite combo: a purple bag of Skittles, Twix, and Donald Duck orange juice. He'd take me shopping and we went out to eat all the time. We would ride around for hours at night, and the time we spent together made me feel like I was on top of the world.

I remember Warren surprised me and told me to get dressed. That day we went on a huge shopping spree and he bought me several pair of shoes. We had matching shoes and matching outfits. I always loved shoes so adding to my shoe collection was just EVERYTHING.

BROKEN YET RESTORED

What really got me was when his grandmother invited us to Massanutten, it was so romantic and relaxing. I can recall telling him I felt like Stella and that I was getting my groove back. We relaxed in the hot tub and felt free. It seemed like we were all alone at a resort in some faraway country. We didn't use phones; we just enjoyed one another.

I thought him spoiling me was a sign of his love for me.

Chapter 3: *Dreams*

Ever since my twin sister and I were younger, we always talked about going to college. We would argue about who was going to be the best lawyer in town. As we grew older, we decided that we should attend the same college that way we could study together and push one another through. Well actually, I felt I would need her to push me through.

Our senior year was a struggle for me, because I was focused on helping pay the bills and on Warren (not my books). My twin Nita was and still is the complete opposite of me. We look exactly alike though, go figure. She was extremely focused on school. She LOVED school, took AP classes, and was passing with straight As. During our senior year, she finished her classes at 10:30 a.m. I had to stay the entire day because I had been skipping science classes since sophomore year. Eventually it all caught up to me. I spent senior year taking science for three of the six class periods. My day was so long and boring, so I left every chance I could. When Nita's boyfriend would pick her up, I'd leave as well. Since he was my boyfriend's cousin, I would go and spend time with Warren.

BROKEN YET RESTORED

One day my biology teacher saw my twin sister walking down the hall and mistook her for me.

"Sharita, where have you been? If you don't start coming to class you won't graduate," she said.

My sister then told her that she wasn't me and in fact she was my identical twin sister, Shanita. She asked if she would please just give her my make-up work and she would be sure to have me complete it all. My sister not only promised the teacher that I would complete my work, but she told her that she would see to it that I came to class every day. That day, like clockwork at 10:30 a.m., I was standing outside of the school's cafeteria waiting for my sister's boyfriend to pull up so that I could leave and spend time with Warren. My sister walked out with a stack of papers and a mean look.

"What's wrong with you and where's your man?"

"He's not coming and you're what's wrong with me," she said.

"Me?" I asked confused.

"Yes, YOU! Your science teacher thought I was you and told me if I don't come to class I'm going to fail. She said you haven't been there for weeks. This is all your makeup work you have to do in order to get back on track. From now on I won't be going home early either. I'm staying here all day to make sure you go to all your classes. So let's go. It's time for you to be in that class now and you're already late!"

ABANDONED DREAMS

I couldn't say anything. I just turned around and went to my locker to retrieve my biology book that had been collecting dust and headed to class.

Having my twin beside me throughout the year helped tremendously! She would constantly tell me, "Rita you have to get it together. How would it look for them to call my name at graduation and not yours? You think you would be ok with yourself if you were to watch me graduate from the audience?"

Needless to say, I graduated that year with passing grades in all of my classes with high hopes of going to college. My sister and I were researching colleges for a while and came to the conclusion one day at work while we were on break that we would attend the University of Maryland Eastern Shore. They had offered us a deal, one of us would pay full tuition while the other would receive half off. We both agreed that we'd pay half of the total tuition and go on to further our education.

One day we were at work at Giant grocery store. I took a break to call Warren and tell him about our plans for college.

"I'm thinking of going to college. Nita and I already signed up and they're going to give us money off of the tuition because we are twins. Isn't that great!" I told Warren as I was on my lunch break at work.

"Actually it isn't, and if you do decide to go, that'll be the end of us. How can I have a woman all the way in college and I'm here. What about me?" Warren's tone was totally different than what I had heard before. My heart sank. I really couldn't believe he was saying this after all the times he said he wanted me to be the best I could be.

"It's not like I won't come back to visit. Plus, I'm doing this for us so we will be straight in the long run." I said to him, hoping he would lighten up and see things for what they were.

"I already said how I feel about this. You have a decision to make."

Then he hung up. I stood there in the grocery store service deli staring at a blank phone. I knew my break was almost over, and I needed to get back to work, but there was so much to think about now. Warren's reaction completely took me off guard. *Now what will I do?* I felt like Warren was the best thing that had happened to me in a very long time. Could I just leave and allow someone else to have him? I walked over to my sister, who was working in the bakery. Nita was in the middle of bagging bread, but I interrupted her—

"I don't know about going to Eastern Shore anymore. Warren said that he would break up with me if I left. Maybe we can go to PG Community College together."

I was so sad. All the excitement she and I had shared moments before had been deflated, but I wanted her to understand.

"WHAT! ARE YOU CRAZY?!" She looked at me with total disgust as she yelled. "HE'S SELFISH."

"He loves me," I said as I walked away.

"You're going to regret this," my sister said, but I paid her no mind.

Two weeks later, my sister, her boyfriend, Warren, and I went to eat at Olive Garden. On the way home, Nita's boyfriend Deuce was driving, and he started talking to Warren and said, "It's time for you to step up to the plate and take care of your responsibilities. You have a son out here, and you need to take care of him."

I was sitting behind my sister, and I was super shocked. I tapped her on the shoulder, and whispered in her ear, "He has a son?" She looked back at me, shrugged her shoulders, which let me know she was also surprised by this news. I sat back in the seat and just stared out the window in silence for the remainder of the ride home.

That night, I found out that Warren was also lying to me about his name. As Deuce continued talking, he said, "Y'all have the same name. That's your junior." Then, he said a name that was completely foreign to me. I couldn't help but think that I had been sharing my heart and my life with a stranger. In that moment, I realized that I had put my entire life on hold for someone that I didn't even know. *What other secrets could he be hiding from me,* I thought. Suddenly, I felt like my perfect relationship was unraveling.

I didn't talk when we got to his apartment that night. I remember he laid on me and tried to get me to talk. I would not say anything so he bit my cheek really hard. (RED FLAG

BROKEN YET RESTORED

NUMBER ONE THOUSAND) I still didn't talk. I just cried silent tears and let them roll down my face. He ended up taking me home the next day and I avoided all types of communication with him. I was DONE.

Three months later we were in History class and Nita had the whole class against me because I just up and left Warren alone because he had a son. I plead my case about how he lied and I was too young to deal with that. The group of people I was around then made me feel bad so I ended up calling Warren that night and we talked until the sun came up. He apologized and said he just didn't know me. He stated that because of the way he grew up he couldn't trust people. He went on and on. He was so good with words. He was such a manipulator. His words suckered me right back in. This time harder than before.

Chapter 4: I Can't believe He's So Controlling

Control foretells so many other issues to come.

Five months out of high school and I was out of my parents' house, on my own, and "living life," or so I thought. Warren and I lived in Capitol Heights, Maryland. His father owned real estate and we rented an apartment in the lower level of a two-story home. We had been living together for five months, and Warren was already acting strange. He hadn't asked me to go anywhere with him in three months, and he had also stopped picking me up from work. I couldn't believe he actually paid the neighborhood crackheads to pick me up and drop me off. His attitude grew worse by the day. He became extremely snappy and had started raising his voice whenever I asked him a question. I tried to fight the feeling of regret and was in denial that perhaps we moved to soon. I just didn't want to face the truth.

One day, I came home from work and was exhausted after a long day on my feet. I was about to shower, so I started to gather clothes to wear once I was done. I wanted something comfortable to wear so I went to look for a pair of leggings. I searched every drawer and then went to check the dryer to see if I had left some clothes there because I couldn't find any of my belongings. The dryer was empty, so I checked the washer which was also empty. I went to check my dirty clothes hamper to see if I had worn them all. I knew I hadn't because I had so many. There was not one pair of leggings in sight. I called Warren and asked him had he seen my clothes.

"Yes, I saw them, and I threw them all out, along with every pair of jeans you had that didn't have pockets on them. I feel like it's just showing too much and attracting unwanted attention."

"Really?" I asked. "It was never a problem before now so what has changed in such a short period of time?" I asked.

"I don't want my girl walking around like that and if you're mine than you can't wear them." That was all he had to say about the situation. Thinking back to what he had said I began to go through all my clothes I had trying to recollect my belongings. I could not find half of my clothes and my favorite pair of jeans, in particular, was gone. I was so sad about him doing this and it really made me think about the fast decision I made to move in with him.

Our living arrangement was still really new, but his control issues were getting out of hand. I would talk to my twin sister a lot, and he would get really mad. He would see me on the phone, storm around the house shaking his head,

I CAN'T BELIEVE HE'S SO CONTROLLING

"Who are you talking to?" he would yell. I'd let him know that I was just talking to Nita, and he'd do his best to make me feel guilty as if I was not spending enough time with him.

I learned that he had dropped out of high school and didn't have a diploma or anything. I went online and figured out how he could get a diploma instead of a GED. He had to pay $300 in exchange for a study book and test. I studied along with my sister who was preparing to take her test to work for the post office. I studied for a week for Warren's test, and the entire time I was studying for the test he treated me like I had to do it. During the time I was taking the test (for him), he kept distracting me as if it didn't matter. I took the test for him and passed it with an A. They sent him a diploma in the mail, and he was excited and boasted to everyone about how he passed the test and now had his diploma. Meanwhile, he didn't bother to thank me for the work I'd done.

I first met Warren's son when he was one-years-old. When he brought his son to the house, the baby was extremely dirty. His hair, face, and clothes were dirty and he was starving. I washed the baby, did his hair and fed him, and immediately he stole my heart. Warren was angry that I had fed his son and did his hair. However, after the first night I met his son, Warren would just leave me with him all the time. Our relationship quickly went from Warren taking me out places to me staying in the house watching his son while he went out. Then, I began taking his son to work with me while he stayed out doing God knows what. Since I worked the salad bar, I worked in the cooler majority of my shift. I would dress him very warmly and get him ready like he had a time card for the job. This became routine.

Warren had also started a new routine. I couldn't even pull myself to accept the fact that he was not the man I thought I knew. One night, we visited Nita and her boyfriend, and we were all having a good time. We were laid back smoking, drinking, and making songs in the studio that they had in their apartment. It was time to go home and Warren just started acting strange. I brushed it off as another one of his episodes again and we got in the car to go home.

Driving back from my sister's house was a blur. All Warren did was scream and yell. He was starting another argument so that he could go do whatever it was that he wanted to do. I wished he would just leave me be and go without having to make me feel like crap.

"Do you hear me bitch?" I heard Warren yell as I zoned back in.

Before I could answer, he was punching me in the face while driving down Bladensburg Road. I slammed on the brakes, almost crashing into the green Mazda in front of me. He punched me in the eye once more. I couldn't take it any longer and I burst into tears. This was the new him. In a short amount of time, he had become seriously abusive. Every time Warren beat me I wouldn't cry until it was over and he was no longer in sight. This time was different. I was just so hurt. So torn, so disconnected and incomplete. As the tears fell down my face, Warren watched in complete silence and when I was all cried out, I dried my tears and drove home in that same silence!

Chapter 5: *Everything has changed*

Discernment will tell you when something is off.

It was a nice summer day, yet exhausting to say the least. Warren and I had been together for a little over a year and things were not going well. On this particular day, I had worked a long shift and was tired and ready to go home. It was almost time for me to get off work so I called Warren to ask if he would be picking me up from work or sending a ride. As soon as I picked up the phone, I saw a terrible vision. I pictured Warren behind a car with another woman. I shook it off and dialed his number. He picked up the phone, without a hello, and started shouting at me.

"No, I won't be able to pick you up. Find your own ride," Warren snapped. Lately that's all I had been getting from him. Attitude and dial tones. I tried talking to him about it, but he simply brushed it off as me "tripping again." It was 9:30 at night and I really didn't want to bother anyone, but I knew my good girlfriend Montoya wouldn't mind coming to pick me up.

"You know I have you sis, don't worry. I'll be there in fifteen minutes," Montoya said quickly as soon as I told her that I was stranded. *Thank God for real friends!* She came to give me a ride, and as soon as we turned on my block, it felt like déjà vu. The vision from earlier flooded my mind, and in real life, I saw him. Warren was standing behind a car, and leaning on the hood of another car talking to a tall woman who had a ponytail on her head. Her body language told me that they were flirting. He was definitely interested in her. I knew by the smirk on his face, and she was feeling him.

Montoya was driving slow enough for me to feel like I was in a movie scene, with my world moving in slow motion. I snapped out of it, and demanded for her to stop the car. She looked at me like a deer in headlights, and put her arm out to cross my body.

"Calm down, Rita. It's not worth it. Don't do anything crazy girl." She locked her doors. "You're better than this. Don't embarrass yourself."

Meanwhile, I was thinking about how to get out of that car and strangle Warren. He recognized me, and had the nerve to wave me off to pull over like I was some crackhead waiting to be served. PISSED, I told Montoya to keep it moving and take me home. When I got there, I yelled to my sister who lived in the upstairs apartment of our house. I stepped out of Montoya's car and saw my sister standing in the front door.

"Nita, you won't believe it! I saw Warren outside with another chick and he treated me like a crackhead!" She stood there shocked. She couldn't believe I had caught him red-handed. I continued, "Crazy thing is, earlier at work, I saw this in a vision."

"Where is he now?" she asked as she walked outside.

"Still there," I said as I sat on the hood of the car that was in the driveway.

Montoya left and Nita and I went inside. I put down my groceries and went back out. A few minutes later, that same car that Warren was behind earlier drove up the street. I could see two females inside, and they both just stared at me as the car passed. They stared at me and I stared at them. It was like we were having a staring contest and the winner would take all. I was angry, and staring them down made me feel like I still had some power left in this situation. Just as they passed, Warren walked up the street with a sinister smirk on his face.

"What are you doing out here?" he asked. By that time, my sister was back inside.

"Who was that girl you were talking to?"

He pushed passed me, "Man move out of my way. I don't have time for this," he said as he brushed past me and walked inside the house.

I followed him inside, and noticed that I had left the groceries on the table. My strawberry shortcake was melting. I hurried to put the groceries away, and when I was done,

Warren came in the kitchen. "I'll be back," he said.

BROKEN YET RESTORED

I questioned him, insisting to know where he was going, but he just repeated himself, louder this time. Then, he walked out of the front door and slammed it behind himself. My inner detective kicked in. I had heard him on the phone while I was in the kitchen, so I went to pick up the phone receiver and pressed redial: *67 240-602-1234. A female's voice answered. I clicked the receiver. *Who is this and why was he calling this number blocked?* I slid down the wall and began to cry. *What was happening? How did I get here?*

The next day I dialed the same number. I had to know the identity of this mystery woman.

"Hey baby," she said flirty.

"Who is this, and why are you calling my man baby?"

"Girl that's my man, and come October you're going to be out of that house and I'll be there. He already told me so much about you. I know your relationship is bad and he doesn't want you. So just enjoy the time you have left because October will be here before you know it."

Furious, I said, "Well, it seems that you think you know a little something, so how about you pull up and I'll show you something."

"Cool, I'll be there in twenty minutes," she said.

I hung up that phone, put on my tennis shoes, and went upstairs to my sister's place.

"Aye Nita, you remember that girl I told you about last night who Warren was talking to?"

"Yeah, what about her?" she asked.

EVERYTHING HAS CHANGED!

"Well, I just called her and she was talking all this nonsense, talking about I'll be out of here by October amongst other things. I told her to pull up and she said she'll be here in twenty minutes."

"Bet!" Nita said as she jumped up and put on her clothes.

We waited outside for almost an hour and she never showed up. Warren did however, but he didn't say a word. He just looked at Nita and I and then went inside of our place.

BROKEN YET RESTORED

Chapter 6: *Be Patient, Pray!*

"If your faith can't be tested, your faith can't be trusted."
- Sharita D. Woodward

Two weeks later, my sister and I wanted to smoke and so we went to get weed from these dudes on a nearby strip. I lied and told Warren that we were getting it from my cousin, because I didn't feel like arguing with him. We got the hookup when the guy selling it realized Nita and I were twins. After we smoked, we went to my mom's to get our hair done. Not too long after we arrived, Warren called. He had been to the same spot as Nita and I to pick up some weed from the same guy as us. I was getting my hair done when the phone rang.

    Warren's voice screamed into the receiver, "I know you didn't get the weed from your cousin," Warren said! "When you get home, your bags will be at the door and I'm gonna f*ck you up!" My sisters and mother were around, so

I quickly hung up the phone and hoped they didn't hear anything. No one had heard him, but my vibe changed, so I'm sure my family knew that something was going on.

I was so afraid to leave my parents' house and return home, because I just knew my bags would be waiting for me at the door because he probably assumed I cheated on him. I was so tired of all these accusations, and I just prayed and continued to get my hair done.

We arrived home and I went down to our apartment. As soon as I walked in the door, he punched me. He screamed and called me all types of whores and sluts. I walked in the room wiping my face to see if my nose was bleeding. When I got inside the room, he pushed me and I fell into a corner beside my dresser. Next, he started stomping on my face and stomach. I curled up so he wouldn't bruise my face, and that's when I felt his fist connect to my face, right in the middle of my nose in between my eyes and mouth. He started to punch me repeatedly, and I screamed, "God please help me!" In that moment, he hurt his hand almost breaking it.

"If my hand is broken, I'm going to kill you," he yelled, and walked away. Relieved, I thanked God because I know He stopped Warren from potentially killing me that night. I got up off the floor, laid on the bed, and cried. He came back in the room but was in so much pain all he could do was lay down. We both drifted off to sleep.

The next day, Warren woke up and started questioning me about where I bought the weed. I told him that I got it from my little cousin DaDa, and he told me to call him. I called DaDa and he picked up on the first ring.

"Aye Cuz, what did I come and get from you yesterday?" I asked. My cousin was already hip.

"Some Yeah, (a code word). You and Nita came."

"Okay thanks, I'll talk to you later."

After that, Warren felt bad and began to apologize to me and asked if he too could go pick up some weed from DaDa. I had been praying throughout the night. After my cousin saved the day, I began to pray again, "Lord, thank you for saving me. Please help Warren stop hurting me." After this incident, I knew that our relationship was in serious trouble. Warren continued to act crazy and become very volatile, and I continued to pray for God to save me and us. I didn't know what else to do. At this point, I felt stuck and humiliated, and I didn't want anyone to know what was happening to me. I was ashamed.

BROKEN YET RESTORED

Chapter 7: *Too Many Battles*

Often times when we lose all hope and think it's the end, remember God, and pray. IT'S NOT THE END!

A month passed and things were back to normal. The fighting had calmed down, and I thought for sure my prayers were working. Warren and I hadn't had as many arguments since that episode about the weed. It had been an entire month since he raised his voice or his fist at me.

The night of December 12, 2005 was amazing. Warren and I made love for hours until two o'clock in the morning. I was still on a high, and I wanted to let him know how much I appreciated him. During my lunch break the following day, I decided to surprise him with takeout lunch to show how much I appreciated the "new" Warren. I also wanted to let him know how amazing the previous night had been. I called him four times to see what he wanted to eat, however, he didn't answer so I just purchased us both a large number one from McDonald's and headed home. On the way, there were so many traffic delays, including accidents, congestion, and construction. I almost decided to turn around because my hour lunch break was almost over.

"We came all the way here girl. We're going home," Nita was my lunchtime riding partner.

We pulled into the driveway, and I was surprised that Warren's car was there, and yet he hadn't answered the phone. I walked in the house and went downstairs. As I got closer to the door, I could hear moaning. *No this can't be what it sounds like,* I thought. The moans grew louder as I reached the door. I turned the knob only to see Warren under the cover and on top of another woman in our bed. My heart shattered into a million pieces. *We had just been in this same place, in this same position just last night!* He had been the only thought I could focus on all day, yet for Warren, it was totally different. He had another woman in our home, in our bed, making love to her. I dropped the food and drinks and just ran back upstairs.

"Nita, Warren is downstairs having sex with another woman," I yelled.

"OK, so what are you doing up here?" she looked at me confused.

I instantly took off my earrings and ran back downstairs. The door was closed and locked. I banged on the door and threw my body against it trying to break it down. Warren opened the door, grabbed me up, and took me to the bathroom that was down the hall and around the corner. He locked me inside until the girl had a chance to escape. He kept saying, "I'm sorry, I'm sorry." He was going in and out and I started to feel faint.

"Open the door Warren, I can't breathe," I yelled.

When she was out of sight, the doorknob turned, and there he and I stood face-to-face. I gave him a death stare, left and got in the car. My hair looked like I had been electrocuted, and my eyes were bloodshot red.

"You look totally different from when we just left Rita, everyone is going to know something happened," Nita said.

"I don't care, I just need to get away from this house."

We drove to work in silence and as soon as I walked in the office, my manager came over to me and told me to go over to the conference room for the rest of the day or at least until I got myself together. "Don't worry," she said, "You'll still get paid." I cried for the remainder of my shift, which was four hours to be exact. It was the end of the day, and when I walked out to the parking lot, Warren was waiting for me.

"Come with me Rita," he said. I just shook my head no and kept walking.

"You better," he said. I didn't want to make a scene at my job so I opened the passenger door and sat down. I could barely get in, because the car was filled with so many gifts for me. I couldn't remember the last time he had bought me anything. In that moment, I could care less. None of the gifts mattered to me. We pulled up to the house we still shared, which had become a shackleless prison for me, and walked inside. As soon as I got into the room, I burst into tears unable to hold back my emotions.

"Shut up! Don't come in here with that because I don't want to hear it," Warren yelled. I wiped my eyes and continued to cry on the inside. *WHY was I even back here with him, in this room?* Warren came over to me and started to kiss me. I moved my head. He kept kissing me and started to take my clothes off. I cried and begged him to stop. He used his strength to remove what I wore and forced himself on me. He started having sex with me against my will in the same bed, on top of the same covers that were on the bed when he had sex with another woman just five hours before.

"Lord Please help me," I cried, as I zoned out.

After it was over, I felt horrible. I felt used, abused, and empty. At this point, I felt like nothing. I couldn't believe he could treat me this way… rape me after I caught him cheating on me in our bed. It was like he didn't want me to process my emotions or cry. I felt useless and controlled from the inside out. I couldn't even control my own tears. This man was smothering me and I couldn't wrap my head around the fact that he really thought having sex would fix everything. Now, I was not only being cheated on, abused, but I was a victim of rape. There is no pain the Lord cannot feel. The battle is the Lord's.

Chapter 8: *No Judgment Zone*

I'm almost certain that no one goes into any kind of relationship with the intent of being abused. The crazy part is that the abuse normally starts once the abuser has realized that he or she is in control and the "victim" is now in a vulnerable state. The initial incident comes out of nowhere, and you'll find yourself either making excuses for the behavior, questioning, or blaming yourself. Over time, you will start to feel worthless. You start believing that you may deserve it or maybe in fact it's the abuser's way of showing you that he/she loves you. Of course, you have thoughts of leaving, then you fall back into that mindset of *what if...? What if he changes? What if I can change him? What if we go to counseling? What if no one ever loves me again?...* The what ifs vary based on the relationship and the circumstances. Personally, I wasn't afraid of my abuser so my "what if" was never a *what if he kills me*. Ironically, my "what if" was *what if he finds someone else?* Crazy right? However, being abused isn't just physical. You can be abused on different levels, including mentally, emotionally, spiritually, financially, and physically.

BROKEN YET RESTORED

I was a victim of all of the above. My mind was the first to be abused. He started degrading my character and what I stood for. Next, I experienced emotional, spiritual, financial and physical abuse. It seemed to all happen so fast. It's so easy to judge or to think *that would never be me,* but before you go down that road, let me share some important statistics about domestic violence and sexual assault:

- Nearly twenty people per minute are physically abused by an intimate partner in the United States. This equates to more than ten million men and women per year.

- Women between the ages of 18-24 are most commonly abused by an intimate partner.

- On a typical day, more than 20,000 phone calls are placed to domestic violence hotlines.

- One in three women and one in four men have experienced some form of physical violence from an intimate relationship.

- One in five women and one in seven men in the United States have been raped in their lifetime.

NO JUDGEMENT ZONE

- Nearly forty-seven percent of females and forty-five percent of male victims of rape in the United States were raped by an acquaintance. Of that number 45.4% of females and twenty-nine percent of the males were raped by an intimate partner.

Statistics provided by National Coalition Against Domestic Violence

The economic impact of domestic violence has proven that victims of intimate partner violence lose a total of eight million days of paid work each year. Between twenty-one and sixty percent of victims lose their jobs due to reasons stemming from the abuse and the cost exceeds $8.3 billion per year in intimate partner violence. One hundred forty-two women were murdered in their workplace by their abusers and seventy-eight percent of women were killed in the workplace during 2003-2008 alone.

Domestic Violence is very real and it happens way too often. The scary part is that many victims like myself feel sorry for their abusers and endure it. We choose to cover it up and protect the people who come close (and often succeed) at killing us. In hindsight, I can speak intelligently about this situation and say that I wish I would have left much sooner. I wish that I hadn't have covered it up or made excuses for Warren, and I wish that I had confided in someone, especially my sisters, but I didn't. Now, my goal is to make sure that no one I know or who reads my story continues to endure domestic violence. If you are going through this, please do not suffer in silence. Speaking out brings liberation and healing.

Part 2:
Thoughts on Paper

BROKEN YET RESTORED

THOUGHTS ON PAPER

In the following section, I've included my actual *unedited* journal entries from this time in my life along with reflections from today. During this time, I was like a walking zombie and my thoughts do not reflect those of my normal self. I woke up, went through my daily routine, and I prayed at night and hoped he would change. My mind was consumed with prayer and hope for change. I would always ask God for a sign, then Warren and I would fight, and I would cry and continue to pray for a sign. It's obvious that God was giving me sign after sign, but because my heart was fixed on Warren changing, I couldn't see the truth of what was right in front of me. I cared most about my abuser changing and our ability to restore our relationship verses getting out and being safe. This is common…

    I felt like less of a woman. I didn't feel beautiful. I was really small, however, I still felt fat. I honestly felt like nothing that I could do or be was enough. I remember praying to God to change me and make me be what Warren wanted. I asked God to allow Warren to see that I was the person for him. I really didn't care about me. I lost focus on my future. I didn't think about what I would be, the type of woman I needed to be for my future or my true purpose in life. I just thought about his life. I knew that I was living and I was a person, but my existence didn't really matter. I didn't focus on me and who I was. I just wanted to change to please this person who was hurting me. I didn't care about my physical and emotional being. When I look back, I see that I prayed and believed in God, but I realize that I didn't follow or trust God. I just wanted Him to do what I wanted Him to do, rather than trusting Him to lead me into the situation where I was supposed to be.

What follows are some of my scattered thoughts from this time. I'm including these real journal entries to help you see the mindset of a victim and prayerfully encourage you to journal your thoughts, and most importantly, get help if you are in this situation. Many stories about domestic violence sound exactly the same. There is a familiar spirit within both victims and abusers, and we can only break the horrible cycle of abuse by exposing it and pulling it up at the root. I pray that you read my words from a position of grace and empathy. If you know someone who is being abused, realize that they need your love, support, and help more than ever. This does not mean control, condemnation, or name-calling. It takes so much for a person to escape the vicious cycle of abuse. On average, victims leave and return to a relationship seven times before finally leaving for good, so if you have a sister, daughter, friend, niece, etc., in an emotionally or physically abusive relationship, be patient and offer yourself as a safe-haven for them.

Chapter 9: Confused... Where is this going?

Date and Time Unknown:

Dear God,

How do I forgive when I'm unable to forget? You say to "be still" and don't question it. To lean not on my own understanding, yet how do I go through my everyday life while feeling so confused about my current situation? I know if You said it, I should believe it. I'm trying hard to stand on your word but daily I feel tested to go another way. How do I know I'm in your will and not in my own way? Help me to move myself out of the way and allow you to do exactly what it is that you have to do. My heart is broken and my soul is confused. I feel like I'm alive yet dead at the same time. I want to see you like never before. Please Father don't leave me. I'm here battered and confused and you seem so far. Please come closer. What do I have to do? Please show me the way!

Your child,
Rita

He met me deep in my despair.

BROKEN YET RESTORED

January 10, 2006 7:14 p.m.

It's been 5 days. I hope I'm just late however if I am pregnant, I really won't be mad, because I would really love for Warren to be the father of my child. I just hope we can make it because I don't want to become a "Baby mama" God really!!!

January 11, 2006 11:38 p.m.

Right now I feel so torn inside. Warren accused me of cheating on him and I've been faithful this entire relationship. My nose hurts and I have scars all over my face and I didn't do anything. I don't know what's going on.

For I know The plans I have for you declares the Lord, Plans to prosper you and not to harm you, plans to give you hope and a future! (emphasis added: mine)
- Jeremiah 29:11

YOU CANNOT GET TO RESULTS WITHOUT EXPERIENCE!

It's all in the mind don't stay stuck in fear!!

Chapter 10: Guide me until I'm sure!

Faith is...

The substance of things hoped for... the evidence of things not seen. - Hebrews 11:1

January 16, 2006

Lord I'm asking you to send me a sign you know I'll understand. A sign that will lead me into the direction I need to go. You know what I deserve. I'm asking you to lead me and I will follow 100%.

I was trapped in a relationship, and I felt all alone. Nothing but darkness had been surrounding me, but one night, I looked closer and I saw a small light. *All it takes is faith the size of a mustard seed, huh?* Well that small light that resembled a star was my mustard seed of faith. I just knew God was going to get me out of that situation. I was being faithful, but to the wrong person—a man who didn't care about me.

However, I continued to seek Jesus who died for me. I felt like I was traveling down a dark road without headlights. I couldn't control the situation, but I knew my destination. And as far as I could see, the destination was going to be bad. *So faith you say! At this point I'm all for it. It has got to be better than this.* **PUT YOUR FAITH IN THE RIGHT PLACE, I reminded myself...**

I was praying for faith. I desired it. I believed that God could fix our situation. However, my faith was in the wrong place. I should have believed and leaned on the truth that God would fix *my situation*. He didn't want this relationship with Warren to continue. I continued to pray and ask for a sign, but I had many. The signs were the many sleepless nights, the disrespect, and the abuse. Those were all signs that indicated I should have left. I should have removed my faith from my relationship with Warren and placed my faith in Christ alone. **Is your faith in the right place?** It's important not to ask God for something that we aren't willing to accept.

I needed to first pray for forgiveness. I knew I had to repent of my sins. I also knew that God would forgive me, but I needed to be genuine also. You see repentance is like washing away your sins. It doesn't mean you can continue the same lifestyle and not suffer. After we repent, we should go in peace and sin no more.

GUIDE ME UNTIL I'M SURE!

I prayed

"Father please forgive me for everything that I have said, done, or thought that wasn't pleasing to you. I thank you for understanding and blessing me even when I'm undeserving. I ask that you come into my life. I repent of my sins, and I make you my personal Lord and Savior. In Jesus Name, Amen!"

But he said to me, "My grace is sufficient for you, for my power is made perfect in weakness." Therefore I will boast all the more gladly of my weaknesses, so that the power of Christ may rest upon me. For the sake of Christ, then, I am content with weaknesses, insults, hardships, persecutions, and calamities. For when I am weak, then I am strong. - 2 Corinthians 12:9-10 (emphasis added: mine)

For God hath not given us the spirit of fear; but of power, and of love and of a sound mind. - 2 Timothy 1:7 (KJV)

BROKEN YET RESTORED

Chapter 11: *There's So Much More Still Worth Fighting for!*

God is within her, she will not fall. - Psalm 46:5

February 12, 2006 10:40 a.m.

Two weeks ago I found out I am pregnant. My mind is going half crazy. I've always told myself I would never get an abortion, yet I'm here contemplating the idea. I'm just so tired of going through the same things over and over again, being able to relate to every song about heartbreak word-for-word. Things have changed a lot. He abuses me mentally, physically, emotionally, spiritually, and even financially. Yesterday I got paid and went to Subway to buy a $5 sub and my card was declined. This couldn't be so I just got paid. My sister Nita paid for my sandwich as I walked to the eating area to check my account. Auto parts for over $1,000 were charged to my card. Oh no I've been hacked I thought just as my phone started to ring.

> "Yeah I charged your card for parts to make my car faster and I got express shipping for $75 more so it'll be here tomorrow."
>
> "Really, before you even asked if I had plans for the money I worked hard for? I'm here at Subway and can't even buy myself lunch. My card got declined in front of a whole line." I said it with hurt in my voice and tears in my eyes.
>
> "Well, it's too late to talk like that. It's already on the way. Just ask your sister to buy it for you." Warren said, then hung up.

O LORD, You have searched me and known me! You know when I sit down and when I rise up. You discern my thoughts from afar. - Psalm 139:1-2

Financial abuse is when one partner in a relationship has control over the financial resources, forcing the other partner to be dependent on him or her. Warren had his own money. He would come in the house and throw money on the bed to count. Money was never an issue for him, but at this point, I felt like Warren had a secret life. He stopped hustling and started to be in the house more and more. He'd sit in the house playing video games with his friends, while I went to work. I would work eleven-to-twelve-hour days, come home to Warren and his friends. He made it very clear that he did not plan on providing for us, or even himself for that matter. All of the responsibilities of our household relied on me. I paid the rent, electric bill, purchased groceries, and I even gave him money for gas and weed. He stopped bringing in income and I was the sole provider.

Financial abuse is another form of control and can take many shapes. Many abusers confiscate paychecks and keep their spouses under control through money. I worked for money and he bossed me around and acted like he was entitled to every dollar I earned. My emotional attachment and hope for the future of our child made me stay. I was never really scared of him, but in hindsight, I can admit that I just didn't want to see him with anyone else. He knew that and knew that I would stay after he clearly stopped working.

BROKEN YET RESTORED

Chapter 12: *Do it with tears in your eyes. Do it afraid!*

So do not fear, for I am with you; do not be dismayed, for I am your God. I will strengthen you and help you; I will uphold you with my righteous right hand. - Isaiah 41:10

February 17, 2006 9:58 p.m.

Maybe our time is up. I'm so mad because I really love Warren and I wanted to marry him. I don't know why he cheats on me. I'm hurting. It feels so bad because he acts like I'm nothing and we've been together so long. I really need to get away and think about my life and if it's really worth everything I'm going through. I've realized it's nothing I can do to make Warren be faithful to me. It's all I ask of him. I cannot for the life of me understand why Warren cheats so much. It's nothing but the devil yet he succumbs to the women and forgets all about me. It's crazy and I guess I'll never really understand why. I'm FED up to the fullest degree. He tells me all the time he hates me. I caught him sleeping with another

> woman in our bed and he STILL cheats. Last week we were at his sister's house and I don't know how it all started but I just remember being on the floor and he was pulling my arms all the way back trying to break them. I know she heard my screams because she was right in the back [of the house]. He started to cover my mouth so she couldn't hear then he closed my nose so I couldn't breathe. I thought I was about to die. I bit his hand very hard and cried out with all I had left in me then she came running out her room and pushed him off me.
> **WHY AM I HERE?**

This entry scares me the most, because I was being physically abused, but I only worried (or cared) about the cheating. The abuse had become normal to me. I would tolerate the abuse and allow my body to heal. Yet, I would focus on the cheating and wonder why he was hurting me in that way. Abuse is not love. Hitting, scratching, punching, kicking, and choking is not love, and it should never become our normal. A MAN respects his woman and will never beat her. Abuse is confirmation of a lack of love. Far too often, we get stuck on thoughts such as *is it me* or *what does she have that I don't,* instead of *THIS IS NOT IT! PERIOD!* I know it sounds cliché, however, love does not come with a black eye.

DO IT WITH TEARS IN YOUR EYES

April 22, 2006

Today I'm 22 weeks and 5 days!!!!!

April 23, 2006

RAGING THOUGHTS UNHEARD EMOTIONS!!!!!!

April 29, 2006

Singing, "God is fighting for us, pushing back the darkness, lightning up the kingdom, that cannot be shaken."

Nobody hurts my feelings like him. Nothing I do is ever right. I'm so lonely. If you drop a glass on the floor, once it breaks, that's me. Without God right now I don't know how I would make it. My whole family was right about him. Maybe I should just swallow my pride and go back home to live with my parents. I'll feel so ashamed. I don't want everyone to tell me they told me so. I kinda' figured my family knew something was up. I went past my parents' house yesterday and it got warm so I took off my jacket. My older sister Sherrell saw the bruises going all the way up my arm and said, "What the h*ll happened to your arm?" Warren had held me down the night before last and punched me in my arm and back for no reason. My whole left arm was purple and black. I made up a lie and told her I was OK, and went to put my jacket on, but she gave me that look and brushed it off. I knew she still thought about it because she's so overprotective of her family. I'm so over this whole thing.

BROKEN YET RESTORED

He puts me down every chance he gets. I haven't heard a compliment from him in so long. He gets mad because I go sit on the PORCH! What am I supposed to do... lay down all day and look at TV? He is outside all day doing whatever he wants to do. I recently had to quit my job because the baby was making me so sick. I couldn't hold anything down. I've lost so much weight, it's crazy.

Later that day.......

Warren is mad for no reason yet again. I feel so unwanted. No one knows, but I cry myself to sleep most nights. I'm so sad, depressed, and lonely. Warren doesn't know because he's never here when I go to sleep. If he did know, he wouldn't care anyway. I just wish things were back to normal. It's hard trying to fake a smile when deep inside I'm hurting like hell. I keep praying to God and I'm not going to lose faith because I know it has to get better than this. I just don't know how it got like this. I have to schedule a doctor's appointment to see if I am having a boy or a girl. I can't wait until I find out. It really doesn't matter to me as long as it's a healthy baby. (God please send me an angel.)

May 18, 2006

All I can do is pray, keep my head to the sky, and know through God, I will maintain and raise my child. I know I can raise my child on my own if it has to go that way.

DO IT WITH TEARS IN YOUR EYES

God please help me, PLEASE. I can't continue to go through this. Why ME? Why must I always be hurt? Life isn't fair! I'm always made to be a bad person and I can't take it any longer. I'm so tired!!!! We were at his sister's house earlier and he snapped. I don't know what happened to him but he just slapped me twice. I looked at him very mean and stomped off to go the back room. This time his sister wasn't home. I slammed the door and just sat on the bed and cried. He came bursting through the door yelling asking me who did I think I was slamming doors around there. He punched me so many times and slammed me all over the floor. In the middle of him trying to kick me there was a loud knock at the door. "Police open the door right now." Warren gave me an evil look and went to the door. The police came in and said the neighbors below heard a woman crying for help and heard a lot of commotion. Warren looked at me and said everything was good and we were just fine. They looked at me. My eyes were bloodshot red from crying. My hair was all over my head from him throwing me across the room by my hair. As I wiped the tears from my eyes I whispered, "Everything is fine officers." The one big cop said, "Ma'am all you have to do is say he hit you and I'll drag him out of here. If you don't say it we have to leave." Warren looked at me again. I looked at the police and just shook my head and said, "Everything is fine." He said, "OK, well enjoy your day." They turned and left. Warren closed the door, looked at me and said, "You stupid bitch."

BROKEN YET RESTORED

Chapter 13: *God Please Help Me!*

May 20, 2006

I cannot believe what just happened to me. It was only by the grace of God that my sister and her boyfriend came home. Warren knows that I'm so afraid of his cousin's huge Pitbull, and guess what, he let him loose in the house. In our room, there's a back room, behind sliding mirrors. Warren and I had just finished having an argument. Well he just finished yelling. He walked out the room and I heard him open the cage to let this huge dog out. His cousin had been staying with us and he allowed him to bring his oversized scary looking beast of a Pitbull. I heard the dog running to the back. The door to the room was farther away than the sliding mirrors, so I ran back there and closed the mirror. I heard Warren laugh, then the front door slammed. I cannot believe this fool had let the dog loose and left. The dog was just running all through the house. I had to pee so bad it was hurting my stomach not to mention, I'm PREGNANT! I'm very claustrophobic so I started feeling light headed knowing I was trapped in the back of a room with a Pitbull loose and he could sense I was afraid. Just then I heard my sister and her boyfriend come home. This house was made to be two individual apartments. The upstairs has three bedrooms a bathroom, full kitchen, living room and dining room. Downstairs has two bedrooms, a bathroom, a small kitchen, living room and a dining room. The washer and dryer are downstairs and we share that. When I heard my sister come through the door, I yelled for her. I remember praying so hard and begging God to please get me out of that small back room then she came. I yelled again this time much louder than before. She said what's up girl. I yelled and told her that I was trapped and that the dog was running loose. She couldn't believe what I was saying. It was a hallway of stairs that connected the separate apartments but both had locks. We formulated a plan to call the dog to her that would give me time to run out of the back room and around the hall to close the door on my side to lock the dog in between both doors in the hallway. She told me we had to move fast. Man I prayed to God that this worked and the dog didn't come back to my apartment. She called the dog and I heard him running so fast around that corner. "Come on," she yelled to me, "He's in here." I prayed once more, opened those doors and ran around that corner so fast to slam the door. "Great job," she said. I just leaned on the door and gave thanks to God for allowing this plan to work and bringing my sister there to help.

Chapter 14: You Cannot Allow Fear to Setup in Your Mind

No good thing does He withhold from the righteous!
- **Psalm 84:11** (paraphrased)

Never once did I imagine I would have to go through this while I'm pregnant! How can you say you love me then hurt me? I can barely lift my arm. My lips are big; my nose hurts. Wiping the tears from my eyes I walked to my dad's car.

"Warren Jr. kicked me while I was sleeping last night. You know how I've been complaining about how wild he sleeps," I told my Dad when he asked me what the hell happened to my lip.

It was so big I could see it out my own eyes without having to even look in a mirror. I feel so useless. I wanted to tell my dad the truth so bad and just go live back with him and my mom. As crazy as it seems I didn't want anyone to hate Warren. He's not a bad person; he just needs help. He loves me, I know he does!... *At least I think he does.*

It's crazy, held in mental captivity. No matter how badly my physical body was beaten, how emotionally demolished I was, I still had hope. I held on to the "good times" from the first eight months of our relationship, despite the drastic change that took place. I told myself maybe it was me. Maybe I'm too ugly or maybe I'm too skinny. Maybe it's because my hair isn't long enough. I felt like if I stayed to please him and tried my best to make him happy, he would change. I was spiritually and emotionally depleted. I was also afraid of being without him. Crazy right? It was a fear of loss and a fear of being judged by others. Fear is not real! It is an illusion. Don't give it a second thought. God gives us power, love, and a sound mind (2 Timothy 1:7)!

It was getting really bad. People at my job would ask me if I was getting abused. I was so tired. Growing up, I didn't see my mom and dad fight. I was getting further along in my pregnancy, and I knew that something needed to change. I was tired. I was sick all the time, on top of being abused, and it was too much. His abuse went from a once a month incident, with a honeymoon (peaceful) period in between, to a regular, once a week occurrence. At this point, it was an everyday thing. I struggled to hide the bruises.

In addition to the physical pain, I endured a significant amount of emotional scars that came from his infidelity. In addition to catching him actually having sex with other women earlier in our relationship, during my pregnancy, I'd come home from work and catch him leaving people's houses. One day, I went to make up our bed and I found a handful of lipstick in between the mattress and the box spring. When I asked him about it, he played it off and said it was mine.

I no longer wanted to do his hair while I was pregnant, so I sent him to the lady who did my hair. One day, I checked his voicemail and heard her on his line asking about when he was coming back over. I couldn't believe that he ended up cheating on me with the hairdresser! She was an older woman with four kids in college. She had a nice body, but her face wasn't cute at all! I couldn't believe he cheated with her. She had been doing my hair for five years, and she'd always talked about how she was an upright woman of integrity. She would talk about how she raised her kids to go to college. She had four kids by four different baby fathers. She would always talk about how she beat the odds as a single mother. I thought it was ironic that she did the same thing to me that she complained happened to her. I had been paying her to do my hair for the past five years. He was talking to everyone and had no respect for me at all.

If you are taking notes, you have probably realized how his behavior escalated. It started with control, then disrespect and him talking to other females (two things that I viewed as "minor" at the time). Then, he began hitting me, he raped me, began to control my finances, and finally completely disrespected me as a woman. I didn't know how this saga would end, but I knew I was on a descending roller coaster ride headed for hell.

BROKEN YET RESTORED

Chapter 15: *Cycles*

No temptation has overtaken you that is not common to man. God is faithful, and he will not let you be tempted beyond your ability, but with the temptation he will also provide the way of escape, that you may be able to endure it. - 1 Corinthians 10:13 (ESV)

It had been three weeks since I left Warren. We parted ways by force because we were being evicted. I had become too sick to work, and of course, Warren had no plans of paying any bills. God definitely moves when we pray. The Bible talks about how he will give us a way of escape in 1 Corinthians 10:13, and this was mine!

So, I moved back in with my parents, which was a must. I couldn't bring my daughter into the world in such a toxic environment. Warren and I talked here and there, and I used to go visit him at his sister's house where he moved. Once I had my daughter, I would frequent his sister's house so he could see our daughter.

One day, I checked his voicemail and I heard a woman saying she couldn't wait to move in with him the next day. Now I knew his sister's lease was ending and she was moving. What I didn't know was that he, his sister, and a mystery woman had already begun looking for new places. Talk about betrayal. So, the next morning, he woke up and started a huge argument, and in my mind, I was done.

I said, "I know you're moving with another woman today, and it's OK because I'm moving with another man. He has a Lexus and his own house, and he's willing to take care of our child."

Warren got so mad and started chasing me around that apartment. His sister came out of the room and told him to leave me alone and let me go. I gathered me and my daughter's belongings, called a cab, and went downstairs.

When I arrived at my parents' house, I was so numb. I didn't know what to feel. I remember calling his phone and blocking my number that whole night. One time he picked up and was telling the girl that he didn't know who it was and assured her she could see for herself. The girl said, "Hello," and I just hung up.

I did not call or accept any of Warren's calls for the next three months. I remember I was in my room at my parents' house singing Beyoncé's song "Irreplaceable," and in walks Warren.

"Who do you have coming in that can replace me?" he asked. I just rolled my eyes and asked him who let him in. I learned it was my brother. Warren said he needed to talk to

CYCLES

me about something serious. He then said that the girl he moved in with had a problem with urinating in the bed. He said he was kicking her out and wanted me to move in. I really couldn't believe what I was hearing. I told him how I was good, and would not be accepting his offer. I then advised him that unless he wanted to see our daughter, he could leave, because I was done with the conversation. He played with our daughter for a short while and left.

Two months had passed and our daughter was eight months old. One day, Warren's sister invited me to her house to see her first-born child. I stayed the weekend to help her out a little around the house. I was sitting on the front porch getting some air when a very small woman came out of the building next to the apartment where Warren's sister lived. This was the same building where Warren lived. She was struggling to carry an oversized Hefty bag. She saw me on the porch, quickly turned the other way, and hurried down the street to the nearest bus stop. I was laughing inside at how shocked she looked to see me as my phone started ringing.

"What's up?" Warren said through the phone. I could tell he was smiling from ear-to-ear.

"Hey," I responded dryly.

He then asked me if I was still at his sister's house. I let him know that I would be leaving her house the following morning. He asked about our child, and I told her she was asleep, so I went outside for fresh air. That's when he asked if I saw a woman moving out of the next building. I told him about the small framed girl with big glasses who was struggling with a huge black Hefty bag. He told me that she was indeed the girl who lived with him, and he had threatened her and said I was next door, and that if she didn't leave in one hour I would come over and beat her up. He also told her that he gave me a key to the building and the door so I would be able to get in.

I felt so bad once I thought back and remembered how frightened the woman looked when she saw me on the porch. That's why she took off trying to run, but the bag was just too heavy for her. He broke my train of thought when he asked me if I would move in. Instantly I said no and hung up.

It might sound crazy, but I don't know why part of me wanted to praise God for an opportunity to be back with Warren and another part of me wanted to bust his head for disrespecting me. I'm not going to lie. It crushed me when Warren moved in with another woman. I had just given birth to our child and he was moving on with his life. Had it not been for my parents, I would have been homeless with his child, and he didn't care. He only secured a place for him to live. Why was I even entertaining this offer?

Needless to say, a week later, I was moving into the apartment with Warren. I wasn't even thinking. I don't know what led me to do this. I was just going. Had I even considered thinking about my future, the first thing I would have known is that this would not work because neither one of us had a job. How would we pay the rent?

CYCLES

It was July of 2007, two months had passed since we moved in. Warren and I were having a conversation about the rent. He said that he was going to buy a car with the rent money, so that he could get back and forth to this job that he was supposed to be starting. I was against the idea, so this conversation quickly went south. All I remember is Warren grabbing me by my fresh braids and flipping me. He had a hand full of my braids in his hand and I got up and ran to the bathroom. I had a huge bald spot on the left side of my head. This time around though I didn't cry. I just went to the room and began to pray. I apologized to God for returning to a situation he had freed me from. I told Him that I would get out *and soon.*

BROKEN YET RESTORED

Chapter 16: *Don't look back!*

She is clothed with strength and dignity, and she laughs without fear of the future. - Proverbs 31:25

A week later Warren came into the apartment with his cousin very intoxicated. I was in the house all day with our daughter and his son. We had no food or money. I was so mad at him for continuing to leave and stay out all day and for being drunk when we were hungry. I felt his cousin was trying to make me aware of what Warren was up to, because he talked loudly to Warren Jr. about how he had been at his mother's house, playing with his brothers all day. I instantly put two and two together. If his cousin was at Warren Jr.'s mother's house, so was Warren. I didn't get upset. Warren came out of the bathroom and told his cousin it was time to leave back out.

I had already told myself when Warren returned to the house later that evening I would try to have sex with him. He LOVED sex. Nothing would get him to turn down sex. Even though I didn't want sex from him, I planned to try, knowing that if he couldn't perform, I would leave him the next day for good. It would be a confirmation of his cheating ways.

When Warren finally came home at 11:30 that night, I went straight for him. I treated him so nicely and acted as if I had been waiting for him the entire day. I tried everything to get him in the mood, however nothing worked. He was drained and he smelled like the strong perfume his child's mother always wore. I didn't need to go any further. I knew it was time to go.

"I need you to come get me at 7:00 a.m. please," I said to my sister Nita as soon as she answered the phone.

"Girl it's midnight and you calling me like this?"

"Nah wake up, I'm serious. I need you to be here tomorrow morning at seven. Go to Mommy and Daddy's house, and get his car, because I need to move all my stuff out. I already have everything packed and ready. Please just be here on time," I begged.

"What's going on? Are you OK? Do you want me to come tonight?" Nita asked worriedly.

"No," I said. "He's drunk and passed out. He came in a couple of minutes ago smelling like weed, perfume, and alcohol. I didn't want to have sex with him, but I just messed with him to see if he would get an erection, and he couldn't. He even smells like sex."

"I'm unplugging the phone because I'm taking it back to the company tomorrow so I won't be able to talk to you again. Just please be here 7:00 a.m. SHARP!" I said.

"Ok I will! Please be careful. I love you," Nita said with so much worry in her voice.

"I love you, too! This is way past due and I'm serious this time. I have to go now. See you in the morning!"

I hung up the phone and finished packing me and my daughter's clothes. I packed the phone. I had everything in the closet by the door. That night, I barely slept. I tossed, turned, and prayed. I didn't want to miss my sister in the morning. When I rolled over, I noticed the sun was rising. I went in the kitchen and prepared breakfast for his son. He was a big part of me staying as long as I did. I grew to love him. In the beginning, Warren lied about having kids, and when I learned about his son while we were on a double-date with his cousin, I stopped talking to Warren for three months. I couldn't believe he would lie about his child. Eventually, we started talking again and I met his one-year-old son. Since that time, Warren Jr. had been going everywhere with me. He was with me so much that people thought he was my son. I would even sneak him to work when Warren would stay out all day. It pained me so deeply to leave him. I cried so much while cooking breakfast for him that morning.

"Hey Rita," he surprised me as I was making his plate. "I'm hungry."

"Here's your plate right here. Come here though, I need to talk to you." I pulled him closer and hugged him for what seemed like forever. "Listen, I will always love you. No matter what anyone ever tells you. I love you."

"I love you too," he said in the sweetest little voice. He was now six-years-old. This was one of the hardest things I'd had to do. "I'm leaving now and I'm never coming back. I can't stay here anymore. It's not good for me, and it makes me very sad. I don't want you to change who you are because you are very sweet and kind. Like I said before, I love you and one day when you get older, you'll understand." He started crying asking me why I had to go and why couldn't he go because he always went with me. I tried to calm him so I walked him outside so Warren wouldn't hear and wake up. As soon as we walked outside, I heard my sister honk the horn twice like I instructed her the night before. I hugged him tightly once more and kept repeating to him that I loved him, not to forget it or let anyone change his mind. Then I told him I had to go and he couldn't go this time because I wouldn't be returning. I signaled for Nita to come up as I hurriedly got my things out of the closet and set them outside while she put them in the car. When we got everything together, I put Warren Jr.'s food on the table, gave him some juice, turned the television on, hugged, and kissed him once more and left. He looked out the window until we were out of sight and I cried the entire way to my parents' house.

Chapter 17: Falling in Love All Over Again

The greatest gift I have received from God was born on September 8, 2006. She was seven pounds and 1.4 ounces. Giving birth to my daughter made me love again. It was a different type of love though. I knew God had trusted me to be her mom. To protect, provide, and show her the way so that she may fulfill her purpose.

I remember bringing her home from the hospital and looking into her eyes when she woke up for her feeding at 2:30 in the morning. I was so scared. She stared in my eyes as I stared into her eyes, and I promised her that I would be the best mother I knew how to be. There isn't a handbook to parenting, however, I knew if I raised her with Jesus she would be just fine. Most importantly, I needed to teach her to pray. *No matter if times were good or bad, pray. To trust God no matter what. To be open to his instructions and don't fix his word to your own liking!*

With the help of my family, being a first-time mom was pretty decent. My daughter was very spoiled and received a lot of love from my mom and dad and all of my siblings. I never needed a babysitter and my family helped provide for us. I'm forever grateful to God for them, because without my village, life would have been so much harder.

I only had one fear about motherhood and that was my daughter having an absent father. I was a daddy's girl. My father was very much active in my life and I was always around him. He always built things when we were growing up, and I was always by his side learning. I learned the importance of having a strong foundation from my dad. He would always say, "Get everything you will need and lay it out. First, we need to build the foundation and make it solid, for without it this piece (whatever it was we were putting together at the time) will be no good." From that lesson, when I was in the abusive relationship, I can recall telling myself countless times, *"This is not right Rita. You have never seen your dad hit your mom. This foundation is not solid, the relationship is not good."* However, I honestly believe that God allowed me to survive that relationship in order to learn so that I could help many other women. That's why I'm still here. Still breathing and don't look like what I've been through. He saved me and kept his promise. Whom the Son sets free is free indeed (John 8:36).

Chapter 18: *The Altar*

And whatsoever ye shall ask in my name, that will I do, that the Father may be glorified in the Son. - John 14:13

As I was walking down the aisle, I knew the woman at the altar could feel what I felt. She knew what I had been hiding behind my smile for the past couple of years. I was about to be exposed. However, in that moment I didn't care. I wanted someone to be aware of this pain I was feeling. For so long, I wanted to be healed. I screamed loudly inside hoping someone would hear me. Yet no one ever did. As I got closer, tears formed in her eyes, "Come to me," she said. "Cast all your cares on this altar." Tears fell from my eyes like a waterfall. This complete stranger felt all of my brokenness. She felt the pain through my eyes. In that very moment, I lost it. I cried so heavily. I cried for what seemed like hours. When I finally lifted my head from her shoulder, she grabbed my face and said, "Now you're free. Everything is so far behind you and you no longer have to fear going back. Just keep going and you'll see exactly what I mean." I felt lighter while walking back to my seat. The church seemed brighter, and I felt better than I had in years. Thanks to God! I began to cry again at my seat.

I started attending this church each week. It was on Gold Street in Baltimore. I would pray to God on my way there and back, "God you sent me to a praising church on Gold Street to get delivered from this." Me, Nita and our children would drive forty-five minutes to Baltimore each week. During this time, I learned how to really worship God and use my praise as a weapon. We would be in church for almost four hours every Sunday. I would dance, shout, and sing out to God. I felt open and free in my relationship with my Heavenly Father. I felt like I could release everything that I kept bottled in from my friends, coworkers, and family through my tears at church. My tears began to provide healing for me. I never really released my emotions. When I caught Warren cheating or when he abused me, he would demand me to keep quiet and not cry. He didn't want to hear it. While I was in church, however, I would cry so hard. I would also dance very passionately for Christ.

One day, the pastor was preaching and said, "You've got a praise on you. Everything that is in you can be released through your praise. So praise it off. Dance it off." From that point forward, I tried to release all the pain I felt through my dancing and praise at church.

THE ALTAR

During this time, I met the forgiving God. I realized that God was with me the entire time telling me to leave, yet I continued to pray for a sign. I felt like I met the God who had forgiven me for not loving myself and realizing who I am and who He created me to be. He forgave me for looking at myself from the lens of an abuser versus who He created me to be. I could walk with my head held high again. My joy was being restored.

As I worshipped God and grew closer to Him, I learned that in addition to praying, I had to be open and listen for God's response. To move when He says move instead of waiting around for a different opportunity. Praying to God doesn't mean you'll get exactly what you pray for, often times you'll get equipped with things to help you through what you pray for. Prior to this, I would pray, but never listen to what He was saying. I'd just want the results that I prayed for. I was in my own way.

Don't worry for it gives the Father great happiness to give you the kingdom. - Luke 12:32

BROKEN YET RESTORED

Chapter 19: Still Rebuilding... Patience

Commit your work to the Lord and your plans will be established. - Proverbs 16:3

Three Years Later

Getting back on my feet was challenging. Babysitting during the day and working at a fast food restaurant at night sums up my daily schedule. I dreamed of good sleep. I went from sleeping in cars, to sleeping on living room floors. I trusted God to bring me through. I remember my phone bill was due and I was down to my last $300. I accidently paid $300 instead of $30, and I couldn't even get a refund. They said all they could do was to credit it to my account. Two more hard weeks, yet I trusted God more than life. For it is He that gave me life. I thought, *I know only good things will come from here, and I know I wasn't brought here to be left here. Only faith from here on out will set me free!*

BROKEN YET RESTORED

I remember one Sunday morning as if it was yesterday. I laid prostrate on the bed early before the break of dawn. The pillow was drenched with my tears. I'd hit rock bottom. I prayed, *"Lord please bless me with a nine-to-five job, and I'll be the best employee in the building. Whatever it is I won't complain. I won't, I promise."* After more tears and more prayer, I picked myself up and went to the computer. I filled out three applications and closed it down for a nap. Just as I was dozing off, my phone rang. It was a six-seven-eight area code. I started to silence the call however, something told me to answer.

"Hello Sharita."

"Yes, this is she,"

"Yes, well this is Manuel from Rapid Leasing and I just saw your resume and would love to have you in for an interview tomorrow if you're available." Without hesitation, I said "yes," and he confirmed the time would be 9:30 a.m. No longer tired, I jumped up, ran to the living room, and asked my dad if he could take me.

"I don't have any money to give you for gas, but once I get this job, I'll look out for you... I promise."

"No problem baby. I'll help you. Where is it?" my dad asked. I told him the interview location, and he agreed to take me. I hugged my dad tightly and told him the job would be mine.

STILL REBUILDING...PATIENCE

The next day, I went to the interview and learned Manuel had three more people to interview. He said he would be in touch with me within the week. Feeling confident, I agreed and left. Before I even arrived home, he called my phone and told me that the position was mine. He asked me to start in two days! I couldn't believe how fast God had answered my prayers. I had laid flat on my face and cried out to God to bless me with a full-time position, and three days later, I was starting my new job working 9:00 a.m. to 7:00 p.m. WON'T HE DO IT!!!!!

I ended up staying at that job for four years. During that phase of my life, I grew up tremendously. I learned about me and what I truly desired. I got to know me and I got to know God. I stopped smoking weed and drinking. I even stopped having sex. I stood up and found my voice.

BROKEN YET RESTORED

Chapter 20: *Watch God!*

Train up a child in the way he should go: and when he is old, he will not depart from it. - Proverbs 22:6

> *God please provide a way for my daughter and I to get food, to pay my rent and electric bill. You know I have ten days to pay the rent or we are going to be evicted. I'm so tired of worrying, so I'm putting it at your feet and trusting that You will make a way out of no way. In Jesus name I pray amen.*

I had hurt myself at work and was out for three months. The bills were backed up and my savings were depleting. I spent countless nights praying and crying to God to send means so I could pay the rent for the apartment I was able to get for my daughter and I. I was so joyful and grateful when things started turning around back in 2013. I had a good amount in my savings so I traded in my car for a brand new car and got my first place since leaving Warren!

One day Warren called crying his eyes out because he had done something horrible and was facing jail time. I helped pay his attorney fees, which was supposedly $5,000, but I paid $400 a month to his mother from October until July 2014. His family was using me this time. They all knew he had gotten married, and they passed out visitor slips to all his women to go visit him. I would get off work at 7 p.m., pick up his then 12-year-old-son, then drive all the way to North Carolina to visit him. I was so lost that I even had his face tattooed on me after he had my face tattooed on his chest. I've since had it covered up, of course. DON'T EVER DO THAT! LEARN FROM ME! I even got arrested going to see him one time. His mother was with me as well. My grandmother had recently passed away unexpectedly. I was driving back from a visit with him, and couldn't stop thinking about my baby, my grandmother! She was the woman who meant everything to me. Before I knew it, I was being pulled over and threatened to be taken to jail. My daughter cried hysterically in the car, so the officer gave me a court date and let me go. I ended up going back to court March 10, 2015 and was arrested for reckless driving in Herndon, Virginia. I was going 96 miles per hour in a 70 speed limit zone. I felt horrible the entire eight hours I had to be there. I seriously started reevaluating things. When I was released from jail that day, something told me to check Warren's Facebook page. He gave me all his passwords, but I never used them because I figured it didn't matter since he didn't have access to his accounts.

WATCH GOD!

When I logged on, my heart sank. The first picture was of Warren and a heavy-set white woman. Her smile was very big and he hugged her from the back with a matching smile. I logged off and paced the floor. I was already not feeling this whole thing. I kept telling my family I wanted to be there only as a friend. I should have never told him I would be with him because honestly, I did not want to be. I would write him letters and send him money just because I had a good heart. In the beginning I honestly thought about it and was planning a future with him. I just wanted better for him I guess. As his release time approached, I wasn't feeling him at all. This was my way out. I prayed and paced, prayed and paced. Then a sudden peace came over me and I didn't care. I wrote him a letter and said I was DONE and I never looked back.

Two years later...

"Ma."

"Hey baby what's up," I said as I rinsed my hands from soap to wipe away my tears.

I cried a lot in the shower, so my then ten-year-old daughter wouldn't see me defeated. I often prayed and cried out to God in her face. I just didn't want her to see me ALWAYS crying. My daughter has grown to be a strong, courageous, independent, intelligent, and most of all a GOD-fearing child. She breaks out in prayer in a heartbeat if ever she feels afraid, uncertain, or simply to just give God praise.

"I promise you that after today, you're not going to have to worry about anything, OK?"

"OK," she said as I smiled and continued my shower so we wouldn't be late for the 11:15 service at Zion Church.

Normally, we would go to the one o'clock service, but today was different. We dressed and headed for church. We were running behind, but walked in as soon as praise and worship started. Our usual seats were right in front. I loved sitting on the front row, however, today it was jammed pack and the only available seats that were left were all the way in the back against the wall. There were two seats left to be exact. We quickly grabbed those seats because they were better than being in overflow.

Praise and worship was so good I cried out loud and gave God all the glory even in the midst of my storm. I remember when the praise team started singing, "Late in the midnight hour, God's going to turn it around. It's going to work in your favor," I cried like a big baby with my faith to the sky.

Pastor preached such an amazing word and my spirit was full. I was ready to take on the week and whatever else to come. Pastor went over by three minutes and said that he had to hurry to clear the sanctuary and get the next service started. My daughter then looked at me and said, "Ma I have to get to Pastor."

"Daughter we are all the way in the back and he is rushing, maybe next time." I said. She gave me a determined look and said, "Ma I HAVE to get to him."

"Well daughter if you must then go right along, I can't push my way through, because it would be rude, so say 'pardon me' and go tell him what you have to say. I'll be right behind you."

"OK Mommy," she smiled so big and took off. I followed her with my eyes and walked through the crowd. She was so determined and she in fact did get to him. She got right on stage and started patting him on the back while he was speaking with another gentleman. By that time, I had reached the stage and told her to wait and be patient because that was rude. Now even though my church is very big, my Pastor still knows my entire family by name.

He turned around, saw my daughter, and asked her what was up. I shrugged my shoulders and told him, "I'm sorry." He then put one hand over her shoulder and leaned down to hear what she needed to say. I saw her shoulders jumping and she seemed as if she was sobbing really badly. I couldn't see because their backs were to me.

Pastor then turned around and waved for me to come over. My daughter turned around with a face full of tears. I was so confused as to what she had just told him that had her in tears. He then looked at me and said, "Sis don't worry, we have you." He said something to a guy that works there and then told me to follow him. When we got to the back of the sanctuary, Pastor informed me that my daughter had asked if the church could please help me. She told them that I was struggling and that we were facing eviction. She also told him that I do everything on my own without the help of her father and that she hears me crying and praying almost every night. I never knew she could hear me; I always thought she was sleeping.

A week prior to going to church, I had asked her father for help with my rent. He never helped with anything, but it was my last option and I needed help badly. He came over to my apartment screaming in the hallways saying he had an apartment before and that he is not going to give me any money until the fifth because that's when the rent will be late. I only had until the 26th of that month to get the money in because I was already late. I told him thanks for getting my neighbors in my business and told him he had to leave.

The man that pastor had told to escort me led us to a room with two other women. They praised my daughter for her strength and courage. They said they had never seen anything like that and that she loved me deeply. They then brought down the chef of the church and he provided me and my daughter with two meals each. The lady told me to write down my email address and told me to write down my account number for my utilities and the rental office number and address of where I lived.

The following day, I received a call to come to the main office of the church to pick up my rent check. I then received an email thanking me for my payment on my electric bill for two months. They said they searched my name in the system and saw that despite what I was facing, I paid my tithes every two weeks. It was something else that fed my faith and those in that room. In that moment, I cried so hard and hugged my daughter so tightly. Three days before I was scheduled to be evicted, I instead received a check to pay off my late rent and the rent coming. I cannot begin to explain the gratitude and joy I felt on that day. I just thanked God for Jesus, my beautiful daughter, and for his grace and mercy!!!

BROKEN YET RESTORED

Chapter 21: I'll Never Leave You nor Forsake You

God has kept my daughter and I. It's been ten years since I've been in an abusive relationship. It took that long for me to finally silence the voice inside of me telling me I could NEVER tell my story or share my experiences. I had to listen to that voice telling me to GO... to heal countless women with my story... to move mountains! That's the intention of this book. I desire to raise awareness and let women know that they are not alone. Don't ignore the signs. NO REAL man would ever hit the woman he loves. PERIOD! You matter and you don't ever deserve to be hit or abused *in any way*. There is no excuse. Stop asking yourself "why?" Stand up and ask yourself, *"What am I going to do about this?"* It's a problem, FIX IT! Don't get too consumed with whether or not it's your fault. It is not your fault. Focus on building a future. The right person will build with you. This person would NEVER beat you down, in ANY form.

I thank God I met a guy that helped me learn my worth right after the break up between Warren and I. We tried to take it to the next level, however, it didn't work. I believe God sent him in the middle of my healing so I wouldn't fall victim to another womanizer. Once his season was done, it was done. It was very short-lived yet informative. God has blessed me as I have stayed connected to Him. After ten years of healing, I now have an amazing boyfriend. We started out as best friends (more about that story in my next book).

I'm an author, praise God! I own my own business, Sharita Woodward, LLC, as a certified women and children life coach. I'm also a motivational speaker and domestic violence advocate. God turned my mess into my message. He never left my side. So there it is. I'm happy, I'm blessed, and I'm FREE, and it's all because of faith! THANKS, GOD!!

Don't give up, don't give in…. YOU MATTER. You have to believe it for yourself! Be encouraged! Get up! Dust yourself off. Look in the mirror and say I LOVE YOU!

About the Author

Sharita Woodward is an author and a domestic violence advocate. She has helped inspire and encourage numerous women who have felt insecure, worthless, or have also survived domestic violence. Her dream is to help women not only overcome, but to thrive in their purpose. Sharita's book was birthed when she attended the Make Them Believers Academy retreat with Natasha T. Brown and Caressa Jennings. She is the owner of Sharita Woodward LLC, where she strives to reach women all over the world who may feel trapped in mental captivity. The foundation of her business is Christ, for without Christ she wouldn't have made it through her hardest times. It is in Him that she lives, moves and haves her being.

Connect with *Sharita Woodward*!

If you enjoyed this book, please be sure to leave a review on barnesandnoble.com and Amazon.com. Also, purchase a few copies for people you love and others who can be helped by this message.

Follow the author on social media.

Facebook @sharitawoodward

Instagram @sharitawoodward

SharitaWoodward@gmail.com

www.ingramcontent.com/pod-product-compliance
Lightning Source LLC
Chambersburg PA
CBHW070934160426
43193CB00011B/1682